Color Me
EASTER

Color Me Easter

13-Digit ISBN: 978-1-40034-071-2
10-Digit ISBN: 1-4003-4071-3

This book may be ordered by mail from the publisher. Please include $5.99 for postage and handling. Please support your local bookseller first!

Books published by Cider Mill Press Book Publishers are available at special discounts for bulk purchases in the United States by corporations, institutions, and other organizations. For more information, please contact the publisher.

Cider Mill Press Book Publishers
"Where Good Books Are Ready for Press"
501 Nelson Place
Nashville, Tennessee 37214

cidermillpress.com

Typography: Epicursive Script, Filson Pro

Printed in the United States of America

23 24 25 26 27 VER 6 5 4 3 2

Color Me EASTER

A Springtime Coloring Book

Illustrations by Pimlada Phuapradit

CIDER MILL PRESS

BOOK PUBLISHERS

Introduction

If you're reading this, you're our kind of person. Maybe you're stressed out from work or exhausted by your social life—or maybe you're totally zen already and just looking for a creative outlet (tell us your secrets, please). For whatever reason, you've decided to unwind with this springtime coloring book.

These delightful designs are suitable for all skill levels. The pages are one-sided, so your art won't bleed through. You can use whatever tool you want to fill in these charming illustrations: colored pencils, markers, gel pens, watercolors, crayons, you name it. Color inside the lines or outside of them—the point is to relax and create something that makes you happy.

However you choose to bring these Easter scenes to life, we're sure that you'll enjoy unleashing your inner artist with these beautiful illustrations. Share your enchanting creations with the world by posting on social media with the hashtag #colormeeaster (and be sure to tag us @cidermillpress)! Now go forth and find your bliss with *Color Me Easter*.

Share Your
MASTERPIECES

Don't keep your colorful creations to yourself—take a pic and share it on social media with the hashtag **#colormeeaster** and tag us @cidermillpress!

#COLORMEEASTER #COLORMEEASTER
#COLORMEEASTER #COLORMEEASTER
#COLORMEEASTER #COLORMEEASTER
#COLORMEEASTER #COLORMEEASTER
#COLORMEEASTER #COLORMEEASTER
#COLORMEEASTER #COLORMEEASTER
#COLORMEEASTER #COLORMEEASTER
#COLORMEEASTER #COLORMEEASTER
#COLORMEEASTER #COLORMEEASTER
#COLORMEEASTER #COLORMEEASTER
#COLORMEEASTER #COLORMEEASTER
#COLORMEEASTER #COLORMEEASTER
#COLORMEEASTER #COLORMEEASTER
#COLORMEEASTER #COLORMEEASTER
#COLORMEEASTER #COLORMEEASTER
#COLORMEEASTER #COLORMEEASTER
#COLORMEEASTER #COLORMEEASTER
#COLORMEEASTER #COLORMEEASTER

#COLORMEEASTER #COLORMEEASTER

#COLORMEEASTER #COLORMEEASTER

#COLORMEEASTER #COLORMEEASTER

#COLORMEEASTER #COLORMEEASTER

#COLORMEEASTER #COLORMEEASTER

#COLORMEEASTER #COLORMEEASTER

#COLORMEEASTER #COLORMEEASTER

#COLORMEEASTER #COLORMEEASTER

#COLORMEEASTER #COLORMEEASTER

#COLORMEEASTER #COLORMEEASTER

#COLORMEEASTER #COLORMEEASTER

#COLORMEEASTER #COLORMEEASTER

#COLORMEEASTER #COLORMEEASTER

#COLORMEEASTER #COLORMEEASTER

#COLORMEEASTER #COLORMEEASTER

#COLORMEEASTER #COLORMEEASTER

#COLORMEEASTER #COLORMEEASTER

#COLORMEEASTER #COLORMEEASTER

#COLORMEEASTER #COLORMEEASTER

#COLORMEEASTER #COLORMEEASTER
#COLORMEEASTER #COLORMEEASTER
#COLORMEEASTER #COLORMEEASTER
#COLORMEEASTER #COLORMEEASTER
#COLORMEEASTER #COLORMEEASTER
#COLORMEEASTER #COLORMEEASTER
#COLORMEEASTER #COLORMEEASTER
#COLORMEEASTER #COLORMEEASTER
#COLORMEEASTER #COLORMEEASTER
#COLORMEEASTER #COLORMEEASTER
#COLORMEEASTER #COLORMEEASTER
#COLORMEEASTER #COLORMEEASTER
#COLORMEEASTER #COLORMEEASTER
#COLORMEEASTER #COLORMEEASTER
#COLORMEEASTER #COLORMEEASTER
#COLORMEEASTER #COLORMEEASTER
#COLORMEEASTER #COLORMEEASTER
#COLORMEEASTER #COLORMEEASTER

#COLORMEEASTER #COLORMEEASTER
#COLORMEEASTER #COLORMEEASTER
#COLORMEEASTER #COLORMEEASTER
#COLORMEEASTER #COLORMEEASTER
#COLORMEEASTER #COLORMEEASTER
#COLORMEEASTER #COLORMEEASTER
#COLORMEEASTER #COLORMEEASTER
#COLORMEEASTER #COLORMEEASTER
#COLORMEEASTER #COLORMEEASTER
#COLORMEEASTER #COLORMEEASTER
#COLORMEEASTER #COLORMEEASTER
#COLORMEEASTER #COLORMEEASTER
#COLORMEEASTER #COLORMEEASTER
#COLORMEEASTER #COLORMEEASTER
#COLORMEEASTER #COLORMEEASTER
#COLORMEEASTER #COLORMEEASTER
#COLORMEEASTER #COLORMEEASTER
#COLORMEEASTER #COLORMEEASTER
#COLORMEEASTER #COLORMEEASTER

About
CIDER MILL PRESS
BOOK PUBLISHERS

Good ideas ripen with time. From seed to harvest,
Cider Mill Press brings fine reading, information, and
entertainment together between the covers of its creatively
crafted books. Our Cider Mill bears fruit twice a year,
publishing a new crop of titles each spring and fall.

"Where Good Books Are Ready for Press"

501 Nelson Place
Nashville, Tennessee 37214

cidermillpress.com